TOP 10 CONSPIRACY THEORIES

NISHI PANDEY

ISBN: 9798649651585

INTRODUCTION

This short Book throws light on some of the most famous Conspiracy Theories of our times.

Although there are many Conspiracy theories, but here we have tried to cover some of the most famous theories of our time.

We have conducted appropriate research and tried to come up with an accurate presentation of these scenarios and what may be the true cause of it.

The purpose of this book is to spread awareness. We do not endorse any of these theories. We only try to bring to you the stories and facts that are available upon research.

All conspiracy theories are just concepts and open for research by any individual.

The main purpose of this book is to entertain our readers and intrigue their minds with some though provoking questions.

CONTENTS

ACKNOWLEDGMENTS

Hi! My name is Nishi and I am a full time writer and content creator. I am glad to bring to you the second book of our Top 10 series. I wanted to bring to my readers a bundle of exciting and short Books and this is how I came up with the idea of the Top 10 series.

I hope that my readers will enjoy and support this edition of the Top 10 series as well. If you like reading the content in our book, then I request you to kindly check out the other books in this series as well.

Over the coming months, I will bring to you many more interesting books with fantastic information.

I hope you will like reading this book.

Thank you very much for all the love and support.

1 HITLER IS ALIVE

Well, this title itself sends chills down my spine. Adolf Hitler is one of the most disgusting, cruel and hated individual in entire human history. While the prominent news is that he committed suicide in his bunker at the end of world war II, there are certain conspiracy theories that say that he may be alive and the one who committed suicide was just his body double. There are different versions of this theory and we will try to list a few of them for you:

i) Hitler migrated to Argentina: The contemporary leaders of Argentina were sympathetic to the cause of the Nazis and therefore many Nazis migrated to Argentina at the end of the second World War.

It is said that Hitler too shifted to Argentina and that one of his body doubles committed suicide in that bunker to show the world that Hitler is dead, while Hitler spent the rest of his life in Argentina while often being spotted in other Latin American countries.

ii) Second version of this conspiracy theory states that while the body double committed suicide, Hitler with some of his most trustworthy men, moved to Antarctica in their U-boats. It is said that Germany was deeply involved in occult and alien studies and that they had also succeeded in creating anti-gravity technology as present in alien crafts. It is also said that they had managed to decipher some of the lost knowledge and technology mentioned in the ancient written texts of old or lost civilisations throughout the world and had even mastered time travel and had created an inter-dimensional portal.

It is also said that the Nazis had contact with some alien civilisations and were getting support from those alien groups, who were helping them to set up a base in Antarctica. This conspiracy theory can be backed by a true incident that happened back in 1946-47 when a US navy expedition set out for Antarctica on 26th August 1946 under 'Operation Highjump'.

Naval ships, aircraft and men set out to explore the Antarctic for opportunities to set up research and military bases.

It is also said that there was no logic to send so much force to explore the possibility of setting up a base on a frozen and barren mass of land. The purpose that an entire flotilla of ships went on that mission is because they were there to find and eliminate any Nazi base, if it existed.

Now, while the ships approached the Antarctic, they were attacked by UFO looking flying objects that were simply too fast and manoeuvrable for the US forces. The US navy could not strike down even one of them and the damage they took forced them to retreat in early February 1947.

This incident solidifies the faith in the theory that the Nazis in collaboration with some aliens are alive and well in a base somewhere in the Antarctic circle. They may be developing weapons, controlling minds, causing wars or just simply waiting for their chance to take over the World.

iii) Another theory says that Hitler and his men had discovered the secrets to open an portal to travel in time and dimension and during the end of World War, Hitler simply moved to an alternate dimension where the Nazis won and ruled the world with an iron fist. This theory however, is one of the weirdest to believe.

2 LOST COSMONAUTS AND SECRET SPACE MISSIONS

The cold war era also bear witness to space race between the US and the USSR. While the USSR was the first country to launch its satellite and the first country to send man in space, US became the first country to send a man on the Moon.

The USSR was a secretive communist country from where information is always censored and filtered. It is said that in its race to send the first human in space, USSR launched many human space missions, but they all failed resulting in the death of the cosmonaut that went with that mission, until Cosmonaut Yuri Gagarin became the first man to reach outer space.

The USSR never disclosed or accepted the reality of the lost cosmonauts and the failed human space missions. But conspiracy theorists firmly believe that USSR leaders did show this madness and took innocent lives in a bid to prove them and their space technology better.

Other than that, there are also conspiracy theories about NASA and the Apollo Space missions. While many theorists believe that the moon mission was a fake and was shot in a studio in a bid to win the space race with the USSR.

While other set of conspiracy theorists say that the Apollo missions were much beyond just a bid to land a man on the Moon. It is said that these missions were sent to explore some abandoned tech of an alien civilisation or possibly to explore the remnants of an ancient civilisation that existed on the moon.

While people may continue to question whether or not the landings actually happened, another set of theories question some weird experiences encountered by the astronauts in Apollo 11.

The astronauts reported hearing strange knocking sound on the outside of the space capsule and it appeared to them as if they were being followed and observed by alien crafts. While upon landing they found out that there was an entire base on the dark side of the moon.

Infact, one of the most famous conspiracy theories has been about the 'Radio Silence' that happened after Apollo 11 landed on the surface of the moon. While the landing was telecasted live for the public, there was an instant when the feed went off air for some minutes. It is said that during that time, the astronauts conveyed to NASA about the alien city and crafts that they could see. While when the feed was on they just went on with the flag hosting and taking pictures that were highly edited by NASA before being displayed on their website.

Although, NASA insists that the dark side of the moon is full of craters and is just as common as the other side of the moon, but various military and intelligence officers have claimed that the dark side of the moon is very different from what the NASA says. They also confirm the existence of various alien and artificial structures which resembled communication equipments and other intelligent structures. Even India's Chandrayaan-1, Lunar Orbiter has found underground tunnels on the dark side of the moon.

It is also believed that NASA and Russia have a base on the dark side of the moon and this base is used as a launch pad for other space missions. Some also say that the Apollo missions attempted to establish contact with the alien race that has established base over there and after receiving a stern warning from them, the NASA guys never returned to the Moon.

Another conspiracy report claims to have grabbed hold of a strange transcript that they claim to be of conversation between Niel Armstrong and Buzz Aldrin. In the transcript, they can be seen talking about extra-terrestrial spacecrafts and structures after they exited the Lunar Module. The transcript is as follows:

Apollo 11: "Those are giant things. No, no, no, this is not an optical illusion. No one is going to believe this."

NASA: "What... what.... what? What the hell is happening?" "What's wrong with you?"

Apollo 11: "They're here, under the surface."

NASA: "What's there? (muffled noise) Emission interrupted; interference control calling Apollo 11."

Apollo 11: "We saw some visitors. They were here for a while, observing the instruments."

NASA: "Repeat your last information."

Apollo 11: "I say that there were other spaceships. They're lined up in the other side of the crater."

Apollo 11: "Let us sound this orbita... in 625 to 5... automatic relay connected... my hands are shaking so badly I can't do anything. Film it? God if these damned cameras have picked up anything – what then?"

NASA: "Have you picked up anything?"

Apollo 11: "I didn't have any film at hand. Three shots of the saucers, or whatever they were that were ruining the film."

NASA: "Control, control here. Are you on your way? What is the uproar with the UFOs over?

Apollo 11: "They've landed there. There they are and they're watching us.

NASA: "The mirrors, the mirrors – have you set them up?"

Apollo 11: "Yes, they're in the right place. But whoever made those spaceships surely can come tomorrow and remove them. Over and out."

Neil Armstrong is said to have disclosed his account of what he and Aldrin saw to an unnamed professor during a NASA symposium.

Professor: What really happened out there with Apollo 11?

Armstrong: It was incredible … of course, we had always known there was a possibility … the fact is, we were warned off. There was never any questions then of a space station or a moon city.

Professor: How do you mean "warned off"?

Armstrong: I can't go into details, except to say that their ships were far superior to ours both in size and technology – boy, where they big! … and menacing …. No, there is no question of a space station.

Professor: But NASA had other missions after Apollo 11?
Armstrong: Naturally – NASA was committed at that time, and couldn't risk a panic on earth…. But it really was a quick scoop and back again

Apollo 11: "Those are giant things. No, no, no, this is not an optical illusion. No one is going to believe this."

NASA: "What… what…. what? What the hell is happening?" "What's wrong with you?"

Apollo 11: "They're here, under the surface."

NASA: "What's there? (muffled noise) Emission interrupted; interference control calling Apollo 11."

Apollo 11: "We saw some visitors. They were here for a while, observing the instruments."

NASA: "Repeat your last information."

Apollo 11: "I say that there were other spaceships. They're lined up in the other side of the crater."

Apollo 11: "Let us sound this orbit… in 625 to 5… automatic relay connected… my hands are shaking so badly I can't do anything. Film it? God if these damned cameras have picked up anything – what then?"

NASA: "Have you picked up anything?"

Apollo 11: "I didn't have any film at hand. Three shots of the saucers, or whatever they were that were ruining the film."

NASA: "Control, control here. Are you on your way? What is the uproar with the UFOs over?

Apollo 11: "They've landed there. There they are and they're watching us.

NASA: "The mirrors, the mirrors – have you set them up?"

Apollo 11: "Yes, they're in the right place. But whoever made those spaceships surely can come tomorrow and remove them. Over and out."

Neil Armstrong is said to have disclosed his account of what he and Aldrin saw to an unnamed professor during a NASA symposium. Professor: What really happened out there with Apollo 11?

Armstrong: It was incredible … of course, we had always known there was a possibility … the fact is, we were warned off. There was never any questions then of a space station or a moon city.

Professor: How do you mean "warned off"?

Armstrong: I can't go into details, except to say that their ships were far superior to ours both in size and technology – boy, where they big! … and menacing …. No, there is no question of a space station.

Professor: But NASA had other missions after Apollo 11?

Armstrong: Naturally – NASA was committed at that time, and couldn't risk a panic on earth…. But it really was a quick scoop and back again.
So, this is a conspiracy ridden field of discussion.

3 FLIGHT MH-370 DISAPPEARENCE

One of the biggest mysteries of recent times is the disappearance of the Malaysian Airlines flight MH-370.

What actually happened?

Malaysian Airlines Flight 370 was on a scheduled international flight from Kuala Lumpur Airport in Malaysia to Beijing Capital International Airport. After 38 minutes of take-off the crew contacted ATC when the flight was over South China Sea. The aircraft lost contact with ATC radars a few minutes later but the military radars continued to track the aircraft for a bit longer and witnessed that the flight was deviating westward from its designated flight path.

The flight was last seen flying over the Malay strait and over the Andaman Sea before disappearing and presumably crashing and killing all the passengers and crew.

A massive search operation (the largest and costliest search operation in history) was launched by the biggest group of nations to find the debris of the plane and the bodies, but no credible evidence of the crash was found and no dead body was ever recovered.

There are many conspiracy theories associated with the disappearance of the fateful MH-370. Here are a few of them:

i. Extra-dimensional portal

It is believed that portals exist on Earth and have existed here for millennia. These portals were used by extra-terrestrials to commute to and fro from Earth and they may even be using them today. This theory states that the flight may have entered a portal and accidentally be transported to another dimension or planet.

Disappearances have been common throughout history and there have been many instances of people disappearing into thin air without leaving any trace. And many times in the past such disappearances have been attributed to the existence of portals on Earth which are either permanent or periodically open and close.

ii. Alien Abduction

When any such disappearances happen, we are always quick to blame the aliens for it and from here this conspiracy theory of alien abduction gains ground. This belief has emerged due to various reporting of alien abductions from all around the world.

From many years we have constantly heard reports of alien abduction and experimentation. But in all those stories, people have been abducted and experimented upon by the aliens sometimes once or else on a regular basis. But in the end always they drop the victim back to earth or from where they abducted him. But this did not happen in the case of flight MH 370 and there seems to be no logic behind abducting an entire aircraft along with its passengers.

The aliens after all, would have far advanced technology than our Boeing 777.

iii. The Diago Garcia involvement

Some say that the flight after losing its path was heading towards the US Navy base of Diago Garcia in the Indian Ocean. And as it is a sensitive military installation, the flight was shot down and its debris was quickly removed to leave no sign of the wreckage.

This theory can probably be true because the search operation took a lot of time to start. And at first it was focussed in and around the South China Sea and came down to Indian Ocean a lot later. This would have provided a lot of time to the forces at Diago Garcia to clear the wreckage and remove any possible evidence.

iv. Lone Wolf Attack by the Pilot

With due respect and with no intention to tarnish the departed soul, I would like to mention another conspiracy theory surrounding this incident. This theory blames the pilot for it and even considers it to be a lone wolf attack conducted by the pilot. He himself switched off the transponders and cut off all communication with the ATC and crashed the plane in the waters.

v. Depressurisation of Cabin.

Another popular theory behind the crash or disappearance of the MH-370 is the sudden depressurisation of the cabin which is not exactly a conspiracy theory as this could have happened due to a technical glitch. The lack of pressure would have killed the passengers while the cabin crew within a few minutes.
In this oxygen deficit scenario, one of the pilots, Hamid may have got disoriented and crashed the aircraft.

But there is not the slightest evidence of this being the true cause of the disappearance.

4 SHAKESPEARE DID NOT WRITE ALL HIS PLAYS

William Shakespeare was one of the greatest play writer in human history with his plays getting so famous, that even today we read about them in schools. He was an English actor, play writer and poet. He was widely considered as the best dramatist in the world. His fame can be gauged from the fact that he is often referred to as 'England's National Poet' and 'the Bard'.

But there is a famous conspiracy theory that states that William Shakespeare may not be the author of all his creations. This theory is a result of the research done by James Wilmot who probably was the first person to say that Shakespeare was not Shakespeare.

James conducted a thorough research on the life of William Shakespeare and his findings astonished him and others in a big way. According to him, William Shakespeare of Stratford, England, never read a book or wrote a letter.

Scholars and historians tried a lot to find any written evidence about one of the greatest writers of our times, but to their disappointment, they could not find much record about the author. And whatever they could find, most of it was very confusing or even fraudulent.

However, there is no solid evidence to prove this conspiracy theory but in any case, it is a pretty astonishing one.

5 AREA 51

Area 51 is perhaps one of the most well-known secret of our times. While the US government claims it to be a simple airbase, there are countless theories and evidences to point out to the fact that this is a place, where the US government collaborates with aliens or tries to re-create alien tech.

What is Area 51?

Area 51 basically refers to a US Air Force base in Rachel, Nevada. This base comes with many unofficial names like: Paradise Ranch, Water Town, Red Square, The Box and The Ranch.

Before, WWII, this area was used for silver and lead mining but once the war began, the army overtook this place for conducting research and weapon testing.

This base is legendary for the development of some of the most covert spy planes of the cold war era. The planes regularly took off from Area 51 and people would see these odd shaped flying objects and would consider them to be UFOs. This is how people started associating Area 51 with UFOs. Atleast, this is what the government claims.

Conspiracy theories associated with Area 51.

There is no shortage of stories related to Area 51. While most of them can be ignored as outright hoax, some of the other theories and the evidences that back them up, really make this an interesting claim.

i) Alien UFO Base: many people have claimed that they have witnessed UFOs flying in and around Area 51. Infact, so many people have claimed that, many people every year visit areas near Area 51 so that they too can catch a glimpse of an alien flying craft.

ii) Secret Military Base: There have been many claims that Area 51 harbors a secret military base where all kinds of top secret research projects are performed.

But the most detailed and trustworthy account of things going on inside Area 51, has been provided by Bob Lazar who claims to have been hired to work briefly as a researcher at Area 51. He says that he and others would be ferried to their workplace by buses through blacked out windows so that they couldn't memorize the path or see anything that they were not allowed to see. He further says that Area 51 harbors reverse engineered alien technology like spacecrafts driven by anti-matter engines and equipped with anti-gravity technology.

His interviews are available online and one can see them by himself to understand the seriousness of the situation.

He also mentions that the facility is comprised of many floors that run underground and each floor is dedicated to a separate research or activity.

iii) In another claim, the conspiracy theorists have claimed Area 51 to be used as a detention center where extra-terrestrial detainees are held and interrogated.

Another whistle-blower named Victor, who claims to have worked at Area 51 gave a radio interview in the year 1997, where he claimed that during his stay at Area 51, he witnessed an alien interrogation where possibly the pilot of a crashed alien aircraft was being questioned.

iv) It's the Headquarters of the Secret One-World Government

Area 51 is also considered to be the headquarter of Majestic 12, a very powerful secret organisation comprising of 12 powerful politicians and businessmen. This organisation was initially created by President Harry S. Truman as a panel of scientists and military experts, but the group later gained power and became one of the most powerful organisation that works under the radar for their own personal benefit. They are out of reach of any government or security institution and are said to be an important and powerful part of the New World Order.

v) They are breeding Human-Alien Hybrids

Although Area 51 is controlled by the US Government, but some conspiracy theorists believe that the Base is co-inhabited by the Grey Aliens, who use the base to do experiments on humans in an attempt to create hybrid species. These hybrids look exactly like humans but have the innate capabilities of the grey aliens.

These hybrids will be used as the future leaders of the New World Order.

6 WORLD LEADERS ARE REPTILIANS

It is believed by conspiracy theorists and ancient alien theorists, that there are many different species of aliens that have been living on earth for ages and even today they are living among us.

One of those species is the 'Reptilians' and they are considered to be one of the most dangerous and powerful species around us. They are also known as the species that has penetrated higher level of government and corporates. They are master face shifters and can easily blend among humans. They control the global politics and are the reason for all the wars and insanity that prevails in the world.

This idea was first brought forward by former BBC sports writer David Icke in his book, 'The Biggest Secret. The Book That Will Change The World', released in the year 1999. In his book he mentions that the global society is controlled by humanoid reptilians and this conspiracy theory has many believers in it. As per a study, approximately 12 million Americans believe that this is actually happening..

Reptilians are the species that are not very fond of humans and want to rule us and make us kill each other for their simple pleasure. They are also responsible for many cults and secret societies that often resort to human sacrifices and other gory practices.

The basis of the theory that our Elites are basically shape shifting Reptilian Aliens, comes from the understanding that in ancient times a group of aliens belonging to the reptilian species visited the Earth. They are believed to have come from the Alpha Draconis star system. The reptilians being shapeshifters could easily blend with the humans. They infiltrated the governments of ancient civilizations and took steps so that they can control all humans and use them as slaves for their jobs and grand designs. They ruled us for many years and also bred with human women to produce hybrids. They also did that to inject humans with strands of their DNA. They designed that DNA to make us slower, weaker and dumber so that it stayed easy to rule us.

The Reptilians also have a hierarchy. As per Icke, there are basically two classes of reptilians:

i) Full Bloods: They are pure reptilians and can change their form and can turn into humans. As per Icke, the Reptilians don't actually change into humans but they wear some type of technology that makes them look like humans. It is almost impossible to recognize them from our naked eyes. However, sometimes the tech gives away a bit when in front of a camera.

ii) Crossbreds: These are not pure reptilians but are hybrids. These hybrids do not know that they are reptilians but they are mind-controlled to extend the agenda of the parent race.

Then there are also different races of reptilians. While the top of the chain are the Dracos, the direct descendants of the planet Alpha Draconis. These are winged albino reptiles. Under them come the Reptoids, who are reptilians but don't have wings but do have brown and green skin.

Is is even believed that the Grey Aliens are a result of crossbreeding done by the Reptilians. It is also believed that the Reptilians are the most advanced yet the most ruthless civilisation out there and no one dares to challenge their authority.

An evidence supporting the presence of reptilian DNA in our body is that during the early stages of development of a human embryo, it looks more like a reptile that a human. Also, the oldest parts of our brain that are responsible for controlling the basic, primal or primary human instincts is often referred to as the 'Reptilian Brain. Furthermore, the oldest parts of our brain which control the most primal functions and instincts is called the "reptilian brain" because it is made up of the structures that the reptilian brain consists of which are the brainstem and cerebellum. However, these similarities could simply be because of the fact that we evolved from the early reptiles that roamed the surface of the earth.

The Bloodline: The reptilians attach importance to Bloodlines and they also drink blood and eat body parts. They prefer children as compared to grown up men. Tracing their origin, it is believed that around 4800 BC, the reptilian crossbreds helped the then humans to establish ancient civilisations like Sumer, Egypt, Indus Valley, Babylon etc.

Another evidence in support of this conspiracy theory is that in many religions you can find the mention of a reptilian God or Goddess further proving the fact that they may have existed and ruled us at the time of our ancestors. They may also be responsible for the construction of complex and impossible looking structures like the Pyramids of Egypt.

7 GLOBAL WARMING IS A HOAX

We all must have heard of the term 'Global Warming'. It is an existential threat and demands immediate action on behalf of the international community. If left unchecked it can wreak havoc on the entire human species and change the world as we know it.

What is Global Warming?

Global Warming is a gradual increase in Earth's temperature due to green house effect. The earth's atmosphere, in itself is a type of greenhouse that traps the sun's heat and stops it from escaping in the universe. This helped to keep the Earth warm and make it a better place to sustain life.

But due to increased human activity, the level of pollution has gone up. With the increased amount of carbon dioxide and other oxides of carbon and nitrogen released into our atmosphere, the greenhouse effect has got stronger.

Now, the Earth is trapping more heat than required and is getting hotter by the day. This is playing havoc with the climate cycles and ocean and wind currents. There are more instances of floods, droughts, cyclones and other weather anomalies all around the globe. With the rise in average temperature, our glaciers and even Polar ice Caps are melting at an alarming pace. This has increased the risk of rising up of the ocean water level and submergence of many coastal cities and island countries.

As more and more countries are getting aware about the threat poised by global warming, there is another lobby of conspiracy theorists, that suggest that the entire Global Warming thing is a big Hoax.

They even go on to claim that this hoax is designed and propagated by European Countries to hurt the US economy. Even many in the US government consider it to be true including the current president of the United States, Mr. Donald Trump, as he withdrew from the Paris

Climate Deal which aimed at bringing carbon emissions down by 20% from the current levels and encourage countries to move to renewable and other clean sources of energy.

The conspiracy theorists believe that the Paris Climate Agreement is aimed at hurting the US industrial complex and to force it to reinvent its entire working methodology and invest huge sums of money to switch from fossils to renewable sources of energy. This, with an intent to weaken the balance sheet of the US corporate biggies.

They have named this entire misinformation campaign being run to gather consensus for climate change, as the Climategate Scandal. And the leading journalist who reported this scandal was Delingpole where he somehow got access to personal emails and coversations of leading climatologists and scientists and politicians. He said that these were sufficient enough evidence to prove that a big lobby is working to promote the fear of global warming among the people and governments of Planet Earth. Below are some of his findings:

i) They have manipulated the weather related data before it reaches the world. They have created this hoax and inculcated the fear of a dangerous upswing in the Earth's temperature.

ii) In a collaborated and collective effort, all voices of dissent and contradiction have been silenced with a heavy hand.

iii) They have also manipulated and sometimes hidden the fact about previous instances of global warming when under natural transitory phases of temperature fluctuations, earth periodically entered hot and cold climate phases.

The reason for doing all this is because the concept and the fear of Global warming is too big to ignore now. There are parties and individuals who are all set to benefit from this global fear.

If the above allegations are true then one is again forced to think about the existence of an global government or a New World Order.

However, this is a vague conspiracy theory and there are enough scientific evidence that the Global warming is a real threatening scenario and immediate global collaboration is required to deal with it.

8 THE US GOVERNMENT ORDERED THE 9/11 ATTACKS

9/11 was the biggest attack on the citizens of the United States, on US soil, after the Pearl Harbour incident.

On 11th September 2001, two passenger aircrafts, rammed in the two towers of the Twin Towers in New York city. Another aircraft smashed into the Pentagon while the last aircraft crashed on its way to the Washington D.C.

It was a sad incident that infuriated America into launching an offensive against Afghanistan and later Iraq.

Some conspiracy theorists say that the 9/11 attacks were conducted on orders of the US Federal Government. This was done with an intention to gain an excuse to launch an offensive in the Middle Eastern countries.

Conspiracy theorists believe that the US government and federal agencies were aware of the attack and they created the right environment so that the attack could take place successfully. This assertion gains strength from the comments of former British environment minister, Michael Meacher that the US deliberately failed to act to prevent the 9/11 attacks.

Further, the aim was to establish a much stronger control over the oil rich part of the World. This belief gains strength from the fact that after the Shale Oil discovery in the United States, the production of oil in the US reached record high and the US was no longer in need of importing oil from other countries. Soon after this, the US started taking steps to withdraw its forces from these war torn countries.

The conspiracy theorists further go out to claim that the impact of the jet was not sufficient enough to bring down the two towers. Instead, the towers were brought down by controlled explosives that were planted in the basement and were detonated at the time of the crash.

Another theory that tries to prove that some insiders were aware of the attack, is that right before the attack took place, there were large amount of 'PUT' options placed on United Airlines and American Airlines stocks, speculating the possibility of insider trading. This goes on to show that either terrorists have access to US financial markets or some insiders had prior information about the attacks and they ofcourse were not interested in informing the public or take any action to avert the catastrophe.

Further, it was argued by Political activist, Thierry Meyssan that the American Airlines Flight 77 that is said to had crashed into the Pentagon on that fateful day, did not actually crash into the walls of the Pentagon.

This can be adjudged from the fact that the size of hole created on the Pentagon wall was far too small to have been created by a Boeing 757. While the span of a Boeing 757 is 125ft wide to 155ft long, the hole created on the Pentagon wall was only 60ft across. This is sufficient to raise a big doubt over the entire 9/11 incident.

9 BATTLE LOS ANGELES

While the US government denies that any such thing ever happened, but there are many instances and stories that talk about the day when Los Angeles was attacked by unknown assailants, probably Aliens.

On the early morning of 25th February 1942, people of Los Angeles woke up to sounds of explosions and aircrafts. Some eye-witnesses said that they could see a large aircraft, one like what they had never seen before and many small exotic aircrafts flying in the sky. They considered them to be of Japanese forces trying to bomb Los Angeles.

The conspiracy theorists claim that the US forces fired more than 1400 anti-aircraft shells at the larger body and none of them could hit it. Even the eye witnesses reported a large, round object in the skies over Culver City and Santa Monica. The object after getting attacked upon, leisurely flew towards Long Beach (as if mocking at us and our inabilities) before vanishing. They are open in saying that it was a small alien attack with a localized purpose. Or, it may also be the start of a covert interplanetary war.

As the military was having constant information that the Japanese are planning to bomb Los Angeles, they claim that what was in the sky that night was just a weather balloon and that they fired on it under the impact of 'war nerves'. However, UFO experts have for long speculated that it was a small skirmish involving an alien craft.

Although, eyewitnesses claim to have seen things in the sky that night that range from a big unidentified flying object to various small planes or exotic crafts flying in the sky, but after all the noise and firing and shelling, no enemy craft was brought down and there was also no signs of that unidentified aircraft.

The official explanation gives no real answers.

10 THE NEW WORLD ORDER

This is perhaps one of the most sensational conspiracy theory that states that our World is controlled by a group of elite businessmen and very influential people. They all have come together to form the New World Order where all the governments and the people of this Earth work as per the wish of the Order.

What is the New World Order (NOW)?

It is claimed by various conspiracy theorists that the NWO is a totalitarian global structure of government controlled by secret elites of the world. They are said to be having their own agenda and are responsible for the formulation of global policies and movement of the financial markets.

They are also responsible for orchestrating significant political and financial events aimed at destabilising the normal world order. They are also responsible for pushing through controversial policies and legislations at both national and global forums.

Their aim to covertly rule the world with the individual sovereign governments acting like mere puppets in their hands while they run and rule the entire world for their benefit.

They are the ones responsible for financial crashes and periodic economic downturns as they control huge resources and these swings are created to help them get even more rich and strong.

The New World Order is a fabled secret society comprising of powerful people using above-ground means with a wish to establish a Luciferian Global government. Many ancient and powerful secret societies like the Freemasonry and the Illuminati also are supposed to be a part of the New World Order and it is their ideology and goals that flow through the ambitions of the NWO.

CONLCUSION

The World is full of conspiracy theories. It is the human nature to challenge the rules of the society. It's our inquisitiveness and our inability to understand the grand scheme of things, that lead to the emergence of conspiracy theories.

But, it is tough to believe, that every theory is wrong, that every evidence is wrong, that there is no evil in this world, that everything is transparent. And this once again makes us think about the same question....What is any single one of those controversies is right?

These conspiracy theories, if proven right have the potential to push our world into turmoil and probably establish a better world after the wrongs have been set right and after the hidden agendas are removed from the process of policy making.